It's CHRISTMAS!

ALL ABOUT THE
THREE KINGS

KRISTEN RAJCZAK NELSON

PowerKiDS
press

NEW YORK

Published in 2020 by The Rosen Publishing Group, Inc.
29 East 21st Street, New York, NY 10010

First Edition

Editor: Kristen Nelson
Book Design: Reann Nye

Photo Credits: Cover Adam Lubroth/The Image Bank/Getty Images; pp. 5, 17 nito/Shutterstock.com; p. 7 MarcelClemens/Shutterstock.com; p. 9 https://commons.wikimedia.org/wiki/File:7222_Adoraci%C3%B3n_de_los_Reyes_Magos.jpg; p.11 Zvonimir Atletic/Shutterstock.com; p. 13 NurPhoto/Getty Images; p. 15 GraphicaArtis/Archive Photos/Getty Images; p. 19 Dereje/Shutterstock.com; p. 21 TOBIAS SCHWARZ/AFP/Getty Images; p. 22 vasanty/Shutterstock.com.

Library of Congress Cataloging-in-Publication Data

Names: Nelson, Kristen Rajczak.
Title: All about the three kings / Kristen Rajczak Nelson.
Description: New York : PowerKids Press, 2020. | Series: It's Christmas! |
   Includes index.
Identifiers: LCCN 2018046365| ISBN 9781725302747 (pbk.) | ISBN 9781725302778
   (library bound) | ISBN 9781725302754 (6 pack)
Subjects: LCSH: Magi–Juvenile literature. | Epiphany–Juvenile literature.
Classification: LCC BT315.3 .N468 2020 | DDC 232.92/3–dc23
LC record available at https://lccn.loc.gov/2018046365

CPSIA Compliance Information: Batch #CSPK19. For Further Information contact Rosen Publishing, New York, New York at 1-800-237-9932.

CONTENTS

A STORY THAT GREW

Do you know the words to the Christmas song "We Three Kings?" It's a lovely tune, but much of its tale is made up. In fact, much of what we believe about the three kings isn't in their original Bible story. Much has been added to the story over time.

START WITH THE BIBLE

Often called wise men or the magi, the three kings are part of the story in the **Gospel** of Matthew. The story says men from the East followed a new star for 12 days until it led them to the town of Bethlehem. They believed it would lead them to a special child born to be king of the Jews.

The Gospel says the wise men brought gifts to Jesus, the child they looked for. The gold they brought showed Jesus was thought to be a king. The gift of **frankincense** was meant to show Jesus was also **divine**. The gifts included myrrh, a perfume, to show Jesus was human and would die.

9

According to the Gospel, before they visited Jesus, the wise men met the king of the area, Herod. Herod asked the magi to come back and tell him about the child. The magi were told in a dream not to help Herod and left without seeing him again.

10

11

WHY THREE?

Because the magi brought three gifts, it has become part of many Christian **traditions** that there were three men from the East who visited Jesus. They're called by the names Melchior, Gaspar, and Balthasar. Other traditions believe there were 12 magi. In truth, Matthew's Gospel doesn't give a number!

13

PRIESTS, NOT KINGS

The Bible doesn't say the magi were kings either, though it was a common part of the story by the third century. "Magi" or "wise men" were a kind of **priest** at the time the Bible was written. These men would have studied the skies, which is why they noticed a new star!

14

THE VISIT

Today, many people include three wise men in their **Nativity scenes**. Some people wait 12 days after Christmas to put their wise men into the scene. There's nothing in the Bible that says these visitors were around at or soon after Jesus's birth! They may have visited Jesus months or years afterward.

CELEBRATIONS TODAY

Many Christians **celebrate** the Epiphany on January 6. Part of this event is the arrival of the wise men. Some Christians originally chose this as Christmas day, so it's sometimes called Little or Old Christmas. It's also the 12th day of the Christmas season sung about in the song "The 12 Days of Christmas."

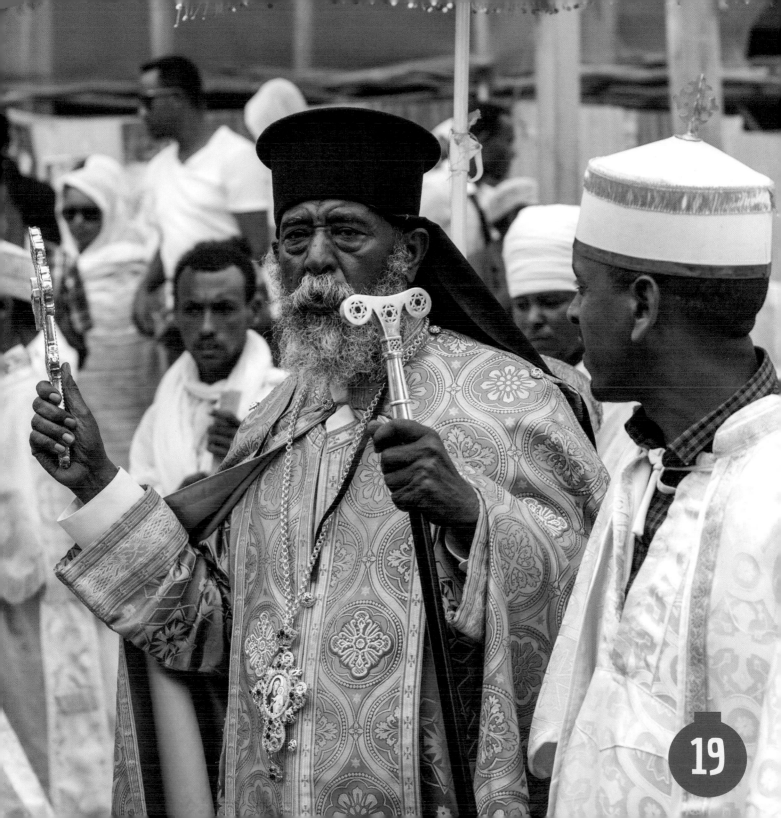

January 6 is a holiday in Latin America, Spain, and other places around the world. It's called Three Kings' Day, or El Día de los Reyes. Children leave out their shoes the night before so the kings can place gifts in them. The children also leave out gifts like grass for the kings' camels!

21

Big celebrations and parades occur on Three Kings' Day in Mexico and Spain and in Latin American communities in the United States. Sometimes people make a special sweet bread called *rosca del reyes*. Bakers in Mexico make one that's a mile long! Celebrating the story of the wise men can be a lot of fun!

GLOSSARY

celebrate: To do something special for a day or event.

divine: Coming from God or a god.

frankincense: Matter that is burned for its sweet smell and often used in religious ceremonies.

Gospel: One of the four books in the Christian Bible that tells the story of the life of Jesus.

Nativity scene: A picture or set of statues showing the birth of Jesus.

priest: A person who performs religious ceremonies in some types of religions.

tradition: A way of thinking or doing something within a group of people.

INDEX

WEBSITES

Due to the changing nature of Internet links, PowerKids Press has developed an online list of websites related to the subject of this book. This site is updated regularly. Please use this link to access the list: www.powerkidslinks.com/IC/kings